HILLSIDE PUBLIC LIBRARY
3 1992 00236 0619

THE BULLY-FREE ZONE

BULLYING ONLINE

THERESE HARASYMIW

PowerKiDS press
New York

Published in 2021 by The Rosen Publishing Group, Inc.
29 East 21st Street, New York, NY 10010

First Edition

Portions of this work were originally authored by Addy Ferguson and published as *Online Bullying*. All new material in this edition authored by Therese Harasymiw.

Editor: Therese Harasymiw
Book Design: Reann Nye

Photo Credits: Cover Torgado/Shutterstock.com; series art Here/Shutterstock.com;p. 5pathdoc/Shutterstock.com; p. 7 vinnstock/Shutterstock.com; p. 8 Tero Vesalainen /Shutterstock.com;p. 9 Sam Wordley/Shutterstock.com; p. 11 Gary John Norman/The Image Bank/Getty Images; p. 13 Westend61/Getty Images; p. 14 MoonSplinters/Shutterstock.com; p. monkeybusinessimages/iStock/Getty Images Plus/Getty Images; p. 17 Carol Yepes/Moment/Getty Images; p. 18 Brocreative /Shutterstock.com; p. 19 SDI Productions/E+/Getty Images; p. 21 Eternity in an Instant/DigitalVision/Getty Images; p. 22 Monkey Business Images/Shutterstock.com.

Library of Congress Cataloging-in-Publication Data

Names: Harasymiw, Therese, author.
Title: Bullying online / Therese Harasymiw.
Description: New York : PowerKids Press, 2021. | Series: The bully-free zone | Includes index.
Identifiers: LCCN 2019059379 | ISBN 9781725319523 (paperback) | ISBN 9781725319547 (library binding) | ISBN 9781725319530 (6 pack)
Subjects: LCSH: Cyberbullying–Juvenile literature. | Cyberbullying–Prevention–Juvenile literature.
Classification: LCC HV6773.15.C92 H37 2021 | DDC 302.34/3-dc23
LC record available at https://lccn.loc.gov/2019059379

Manufactured in the United States of America

Some of the images in this book illustrate individuals who are models. The depictions do not imply actual situations or events.

CPSIA Compliance Information: Batch #CSPK20. For Further Information contact Rosen Publishing, New York, New York at 1-800-237-9932.

CONTENTS

BULLIES AND BULLYING

Do you know what a bully is? A bully is someone who hurts, teases, **embarrasses**, or **harasses** another person. A bully may **threaten** to harm the person too. Often these actions need to happen more than once to be called bullying, but not always.

There's more than one kind of bully. Verbal bullies use words to hurt others. Physical bullies use their bodies to hurt others. Social bullies get others to leave someone out of activities or groups on purpose. There are bullies who use **technology** to do harm too. Online bullies are sometimes called cyberbullies.

IN THE ZONE

In 2019, UNICEF (United Nations Children's Fund) reported that one out of every three children has been bullied online.

People often think of bullying as physical harm. Cyberbullying is a big problem in today's world too.

CYBERBULLYING

Cyberbullies use email, texts, **apps**, online games, and **social networks** to bully victims. They send, post, or share mean, harmful, or false messages and pictures. Cyberbullying is often used to embarrass others. It can harm their reputations, or how others view them.

People may bully online to get back at those who bully them in school. They can do this without even seeing the person. Sometimes, people bully because they think what they're sharing is funny. Bullies may also like the feeling of power they get when cyberbullying. No matter why someone bullies, it's always wrong.

IN THE ZONE

Online bullying can be **challenging** to stop. The bully and the victim don't need to live near each other or even know each other.

COMMON PLACES FOR CYBERBULLYING

- social networks
- text messages
- instant messages
- emails
- online games

According to a 2019 study, smartphones are the most common tool used to bully others online.

THE DAMAGE DONE

Fighting cyberbullying has some challenges. One is that the victim can't walk away. The bully's messages may remain online until they're removed. Cyberbullying can happen any time and any place, not just in school. Many people may be able to view what's online too.

Some cyberbullies are anonymous, which means the victims don't even know their names.

Online bullying has serious effects. Kids who are bullied often become sad and **depressed**. They may withdraw from friends and activities. Fear and worry may take over their thoughts. Their grades may drop, and they may miss school. The sad feelings and harmful effects can stay with the victim long after the bullying stops.

FIRST, IGNORE

When someone is bullied in person, sometimes telling the bully to stop may end the bullying. However, for cyberbullying, it's always better to **ignore** the bully. Replying in anger could get you in a lot of trouble. In fact, the bully might use your reply to make it seem like you are the bully. The bully also might use your reply to bully you more and get you even angrier. Bullies hope for **reactions** like this.

However, ignoring a bully doesn't mean you can't fight back. You just need to do it in a different, smarter way.

IN THE ZONE

If you see cyberbullying online, don't share it with friends. That's what the bully wants.

You may be upset if you're being cyberbullied. However, the best way to fight back is to keep your cool and get to work.

THEN, FIGHT BACK

To fight a cyberbully, tell a trusted adult what's happening first. Together, print or save all proof of the bullying. This is important in case the bully tries to remove it. Next, if possible, block the bully so they can't contact you. Finally, report the bullying to the website, app, or online network you're using.

To prevent future bullying, have a parent help you check the privacy settings on all your apps and social network sites. This limits the people who can send you messages. Keep all "buddy lists" private so a bully won't know when you're online.

IN THE ZONE

Make sure you don't share any passwords or personal facts about yourself online, such as your last name or where you live. A bully could use this against you.

Social network sites often have rules that don't allow users to bully others. When you sign up to use them, you promise to obey their rules.

Sometimes, cyberbullying may go beyond an app or website. A bully may use many places on the internet to find you. You may have to report this problem to the internet provider.

IN THE ZONE

Some kinds of cyberbullying are against the law. The police should be called if someone thinks they're in danger.

Cell phone and internet providers know that their technology is used for bullying. They make it easy to contact them about it.

If the bullying is done through texts, you can block the number. You can also get in touch with your phone service for help. Providers have ways of letting you report threats and harassment. Your trusted adult can help you find a way to get in touch with these providers.

If an online bully threatens to hurt you at all, report this kind of bullying to the police right away. It's illegal.

DON'T BE A BYSTANDER

People who see bullying happen but don't do anything are called bystanders. Bystanders may seem like they're supporting the bullying because they don't act against it. In fact, many bystanders are worried they'll be bullied if they stick up for someone being bullied.

However, bystanders can help someone being cyberbullied without angering the bully. They can tell the bully they don't agree. They can say nice things about the victim. They can also send a private message and encourage the victim to report the bully. Bystanders can also tell an adult what they see and report the bullying themselves.

If you know the person being bullied online, give them support in person. You could also offer to stay offline with them for a time.

BUILDING SELF-ESTEEM

There's still work to do after the cyberbullying has ended. After a time of being bullied, the victim may have low self-esteem. Self-esteem is the way people feel about themselves. A person being mean to us can tear down our self-esteem, but it can be built up again.

Counselors are trained to listen and give advice. They're good at helping people understand and deal with their feelings. Many schools have counselors.

It's important to remember that bullying isn't ever the victim's fault. If you are having trouble dealing with feelings of sadness or anger, you may want to speak with a counselor. Counselors can also suggest ways to make you feel good about yourself, such as joining a club and making new friends.

TECH TOOLS TODAY

Technology is a necessary tool for all ages. Young people need their phones to text their parents for a ride home. They may use tablets in the classroom. Perhaps they do homework on a laptop. Technology has also become a way to play and keep in touch with friends.

However, it's important to realize that some people use technology to hurt others. Many social networks, games, and apps have rules about how old someone must be to use them. These rules are put in place to keep young people safe. Always ask an adult before signing up for anything online.

IN THE ZONE

Schools can punish bullying that's done on school grounds. In some places, schools can also act if cyberbullying makes the school a hostile, or unfriendly, place to be for victims.

Technology is useful—and fun! Unfortunately, some people try to ruin the fun for others.

YOUR ONLINE COMMUNITY

Think of spending time online like spending time in a community. The more respectful and **empathetic** people are, the nicer it is to spend time in that place. In fact, it may take a little extra work to make sure no one thinks you're being unkind online. Words can sometimes be misunderstood.

No one deserves to be bullied, online or offline. It doesn't matter what they look or act like. We don't have to be friends with everyone, but we do need to treat everyone with respect. If everyone treated others as they would like to be treated, we could end bullying.

GLOSSARY

app: Short for application. A computer or smartphone program that is made to perform certain tasks.

challenging: Demanding, or a test of one's skills.

depressed: Feeling sad, hopeless, or unimportant.

embarrass: To cause somebody to be ashamed or ill at ease.

empathetic: Feeling like one understands and shares in another person's experiences and emotions.

harass: To continue to bother or attack someone.

ignore: To do nothing about or in response to something. Also, to pretend not to notice.

reaction: The way someone acts or feels in response to something that happens.

social network: A website or other app that lets users communicate by posting comments, messages, and images.

technology: A machine, piece of equipment, or method created by science and engineering to be useful or to solve problems.

threaten: To say that you will harm someone, often to get something.

INDEX

WEBSITES

Due to the changing nature of Internet links, PowerKids Press has developed an online list of websites related to the subject of this book. This site is updated regularly. Please use this link to access the list: www.powerkidslinks.com/bullyfree/online